MEND YOUR OWN CHINA AND GLASS

Cover illustration: A Japanese Imari plate (diameter 22 in.) broken in 11 pieces. (From Goodwood House by courtesy of the Trustees.)

Fig. 1 Japanese Imari plate after mending. (From Goodwood House by courtesy of the Trustees.)

MEND YOUR OWN CHINA AND GLASS

Susan Wells

IMPOSSIBLE

A hateful word, usually supplanted among
good seamen by 'We'll try'.
The Sailor's Word Book (Smyth)

LONDON: G. BELL & SONS LTD.

Contents

Contents

Foreword

John P. Cushion

Miss Wells appears to have supplied the answer to one of the questions most frequently asked of museum personnel, that is 'How can I get my china repaired?', and what better answer is there than 'Why not do it yourself?' Professional ceramic repairs can be extremely expensive, often costing far more than the piece is actually worth in terms of cash, but many treasured objects have a sentimental value which cannot be measured in this way, but which at the same time does not justify the outlay of large sums of money.

In this volume Susan Wells explains in easily understood language the various techniques, necessary tools and materials required to enable any practical person at least to repair his own pottery, porcelain or glass objects to an acceptable standard. The newcomer in the field must not expect to compete immediately with some of the outstanding ceramic repairers, whose work can often be dangerously deceptive to the unwary purchaser. A certain dealer I once knew was only interested in repairs which were impossible to detect by eye, and he was obviously passing such finely repaired wares on to unsuspecting collectors as being in mint condition. The secret here often being a great deal of overpainting beyond the extent of the damage, a practice the author so rightly condemns.

I regret I cannot condone Miss Wells' final paragraph, where she suggests that payment for repairs carried out for friends might take the form of beer or champagne, which would probably have the repairer in a constant state of inebriation, which is hardly conducive to good repairs!

Fig. 2 The author at work. (See page 19.)

Introduction

When I was first invited to demonstrate china mending, I knew that my students would ask me to recommend a book on the subject that would be suitable in both price and contents for beginners. I knew of no such book and accordingly I wrote some notes to accompany each lecture. This present book is a combination of my lectures and those notes. I hope it will be of use to other would-be china menders, whether they want just to mend their own precious bits and pieces or whether they want to be more ambitious and start a small business.

I find that most people have no idea of how much there is to know about china mending. An elderly gentleman visited me in my workshop one day when everything had gone wrong and I was becoming more and more frantic. I poured out my troubles to him and at the end of my tirade, all he said was: 'Never mind, dear, it keeps you out of mischief.' That is exactly how most people regard china mending – a nice comfortable little hobby which can be learnt in a weekend and which helps you pass the time.

China mending, of course, is (or should be) very much more than that. It is undoubtedly very fascinating and absorbing, and it can be a most satisfying experience when a dirty jumble of broken pieces is converted into a shining piece of china that looks as if it had just come from its maker; but china mending is also plain hard work, sometimes requiring physical strength and always requiring infinite patience and self-discipline. China menders need to use their brains just as much as their hands; they should never stop learning or trying out new methods and materials. While they should always aim for perfection in their results, they must also learn to accept that at times it is just not possible to disguise the mended part completely.

I have been mending now for some 20 years, during which time my customers have ranged quite literally from a dustman to a duchess. In all those years only one has been disagreeable and I have made countless friends.

If the foregoing words give the impression that china mending is more pain than pleasure, this is quite unintentional and the would-be china mender should not be put off. My only wish is to instil a high standard of craftsmanship, but this cannot be achieved unless the mender is also enjoying him/herself, as indeed I have done over the last 20 years.

Finally, let me encourage those of my readers who may think that special qualifications and skills are needed before one can be a really proficient china mender, by saying that apart from a great deal of trial and error, my only training has been 4 days with a master craftsman, matched with a love of using my hands and a stubborn streak in my nature that won't admit defeat!

SUSAN WELLS

General Instructions and a Few Suggestions

When you are mending china, do please always observe the following precautions:

1 Always work in a well-ventilated room.
2 Always read and obey any warnings on the containers of any materials used.
3 Do get in the habit of putting the stopper or lid back on a container directly you have used it.

These precautions are necessary because some of the materials that I recommend, e.g. solvents, adhesives and paints, although quite safe if properly used, can be harmful if wrongly handled. Some notable examples are:

Acetone which is *very* inflammable.
Carbon tetrachloride which should not be inhaled.
Polystrippa which should not come in contact with the skin.
Methylated spirits and acetone which will evaporate, and Chintex paint which will 'gel' if left uncovered.

Although the risk is regarded as being slight, would-be china menders (particularly those with sensitive skins) should read the warning regarding dermatitis that accompanies all packs of epoxy adhesives. Methylated spirits will remove epoxy adhesive from your hands but as it removes the natural grease as well, it is better to use a special cleanser such as Kerocleanse.

Use meths to clean epoxy adhesive off your tools and equipment before it has set.

Knives, gravers and chisels should be kept sharp by means of a grinding wheel and/or whetstone. Files that have become clogged with epoxy 'putty' (see Chapter 3) can be cleaned with Nitromors or Polystrippa.

Inevitably the mender will one day have an accident and break the china that he or she is repairing, in a new place. This is usually a shattering experience in more ways than one and your instinct will probably be to mend the new break(s) as soon as possible.

This urge should however be resisted until you have regained your composure before attempting it.

It is impossible to safeguard yourself completely against such accidents but it does help if you avoid doing any work when you are tired or preoccupied with other matters, and if you take no chances in the handling or the storing of the china whilst it is undergoing repairs.

If you assemble all your tools and equipment for the job in hand on a tray (preferably one with a rim) it will serve as a mobile workbench and you can carry on with your mending in the bosom of your family instead of shutting yourself away in a spare room!

New materials which are of use in china mending are being produced all the time, and some of those mentioned in the following pages may well have been superseded by the time you read this. I can but outline the needs for each process and recommend those materials that I have tested and found satisfactory; but, armed with the knowledge of what is required, menders should at all times be on the lookout for an even better material or tool to help them towards their ultimate aim of the invisible repair.

1 *Cleaning China*

Before starting to stick any china, you must first ensure that the broken edges are as clean as possible – that all old glue, grease and general dirt have been removed. This cleaning is necessary for two reasons: First, the epoxy adhesives (which are recommended for use) will not adhere if applied to dirty or greasy surfaces, and second, dirt, old glue and grease will not only make the break show up much more but will also prevent a really close join. It is important to remove even the tiniest flake, and as some adhesives are invisible to the naked eye, it may be necessary for you to scrutinize the edges with a magnifying glass or watchmaker's eyeglass. A watchmaker's eyeglass needs a little getting used to, but as it leaves both hands free, it is preferable to a magnifying glass. It is also inexpensive, looks rather impressive to one's family, and can be useful to china menders in many other ways.

Methods of Cleaning

If the break is a new one, you need do nothing by way of preparation except wipe the edges with a white (or colourfast) silk rag dipped in meths. Silk is not easily come by these days but is preferable to cotton as it leaves no fluff. This will remove any grease that the china may have acquired from being handled.

If the break is an old one, the cleansers to use are:

For *general dust, dirt and old glue* – hot water and washing-up detergent. If the old glue is very stubborn, put the china in warm water and detergent and bring it gently to the boil, remembering that it is not the actual temperature that causes the china to break but the differences of temperature such as are easily caused by heating or cooling too quickly. But beware of any cracks in the china as these would probably be made worse in the process. Beware also of previously mended china which you do not want to re-do as it might not stand up to the hot water treatment.

For *stains*, stained china should be immersed in neat household bleach and left there for as long as necessary, but you must keep an eye on any gold decoration, as this could be affected. Wash bleach off on completion. If the stain has been caused by grease which has seeped right into the china leaving a grey mark, it may be impossible to remove it, in which case you can only clean the edges as best you can and hope that the grease will not affect the mend. Soft paste china will sometimes show a tidemark where the water has soaked in during washing but this should disappear when the china is completely dry. Hydrochloric acid is also most effective on some stains, particularly those of metallic origin, but this is a very powerful liquid which could etch the glaze (and your skin) and should only be used with great care.

For *stubborn adhesives*, pure acetone (not nail varnish remover which usually contains oil) will remove most adhesives. Rub it on with a clean white rag. It is possible to immerse the china in acetone, but as acetone evaporates quite rapidly, this can be expensive, unless you exclude all the air. You can exclude air from small pieces of china by putting them in a screw-top jar.

For *grease*, meths is a grease remover, but carbon tetrachloride (which is the basis of most clothes cleaners) is recommended for really greasy breaks.

For *epoxy adhesives*, dissolve with Nitromors or Polystrippa paint stripper. Nitromors is available in two forms: as a liquid in a yellow tin and in a glutinous form in a green tin. I prefer the latter as it can be painted on with a brush. Polystrippa is also glutinous. When a bad join needs to be undone, time must be allowed for the solvent to penetrate. This time will vary considerably, and may in some cases be as long as 2 weeks.

Cleaning a Crack

Immerse in bleach, or soak pads of cotton wool in bleach and lay along the crack, re-soaking them as necessary. You can also open a crack slightly by inserting the edge of a razor blade very gently in the top of the crack. This forces the crack apart and enables the cleanser to penetrate more deeply. However you must proceed very carefully or your piece of cracked china will become a piece of broken china. You must also take care not to let the bleach come in contact with the razor blade, or it will cause rust and you will be left with a worse stain than before.

Finally, remember to wash off any solvent before trying another one and always dry the china thoroughly before sticking it. In the case of porous earthenware or pottery that has been immersed in water, this may take some hours; alternatively it can be put in a low oven to dry out.

Tools

For general cleaning:

1 A foam rubber sponge.
2 A soft brush – an old shaving brush is particularly good and a hairdresser's neck brush could be useful.
3 An old tooth brush.
4 Pipe cleaners for awkward nooks and crannies.

For scraping off old glues:

1 Razor blades – these can be used in a safety holder or not as the mender prefers. I prefer them without a holder as they can then be bent as required.
2 A craft knife, sharp penknife or home-made chisel. Details on how to make the latter are given in Chapter 3.

When using any of these tools you must be careful not to remove any of the china with the old glue, particularly the outer glaze covering, as this will prevent your getting a close and invisible join.

Removing Rivets

Very often rivets are so loose that they almost fall out, or at the worst, all that is needed is a gentle prising with a fine penknife blade. When they prove more stubborn, saw gently through the middle of each rivet with a fine hacksaw blade and then carefully remove the two pieces of wire with small tweezers. It is quite easy to chip the china during this operation, so proceed carefully.

SUMMARY OF CHAPTER 1 ON CLEANING CHINA

If clean, wipe over with meths.

If dirty, use one or all of the following:

(*a*) Hot water and detergent for general dirt and old glue.

(*b*) Parazone for stubborn stains.

(*c*) Acetone to remove old adhesives (except epoxy adhesives).

(*d*) Carbon tetrachloride to remove grease.

(*e*) Nitromors or Polystrippa paint stripper to dissolve epoxy adhesives.

Tools

Foam rubber sponge.

Eyeglass or magnifying glass.

Razor blade, craft knife or home-made chisel.

Soft brush, shaving brush, old tooth brush.

Pipe cleaners.

Warnings

Beware of removing edges of glaze when scraping off old glue.

Avoid inhaling solvents in general and always work in well-ventilated room.

Acetone is very inflammable and evaporates if bottle is left unstoppered.

If china has been immersed in water for any length of time, it must be thoroughly dried out before sticking.

Cleaning China

Item	*Stockists and/or Notes**
Washing-up liquid detergent	
Bleach	
Razor blade or small sharp knife	
Soft brush	
Cotton or Silk rag	
Pipe cleaners	
Magnifying glass or watchmaker's eyeglass	Optician
Acetone	} Chemist
Carbon tetrachloride	
Meths	} Paintshop or Ironmongers
Nitromors or Polystrippa	

For Removing Rivets
Penknife with small blade
Small tweezers
Fine hacksaw

* Where an item recurs, the stockist and/or amplifying note is not repeated.

2 Sticking

Before starting work make sure that you have the following conditions:

1 Warm room, warm china.
2 Clean china, clean hands.
3 Dry china.

The reasons for this are fairly obvious: the warmth will make the adhesive more runny and therefore easier for you to spread thinly and thus achieve a close join. If the adhesive and hardener are stiff, heat the tubes gently by a radiator before you mix them. Overmuch or prolonged heating of the mixed adhesive might cause it to set before you are ready for it to do so. For the same reason, only warm – do not overheat – the china in a low oven or on a radiator. As I said in the last chapter, cleanliness is necessary for a safe, close join, and it is extraordinary how even slightly grubby hands will rub dirt into the break, particularly if you are a slightly agitated beginner.

Preparations

Now you must make some preparations before you can actually start to stick. First decide on a suitable restbed for the piece of china while the adhesive is setting. Your aim is to get the two broken pieces as close as possible to each other, so you let the forces of gravity assist you here and arrange some form of support so that the one fragment will balance on the other. For instance, a plate broken in half and lying flat on a table would tend to gape, but if one half was supported with the other balancing correctly on top, the weight of the top half bearing down on the lower would help to squeeze out any excess adhesive and thus achieve a close join. There are many different kinds of supports and it is impossible for me to suggest more than a few, but the ingenuity that a china mender must always possess comes into play here. For plates, saucers and tiles, a plate rack is usually ideal (see Fig. 3), but the angle of slant may have to be adjusted in some cases.

You can do this with lumps of Plasticine in the section of the rack or by propping up one end of the rack itself. A sand tray is another useful piece of equipment. Mine is an old baking tin half filled with pet bird sand. In it you can prop the smaller articles or pieces of a multiple break at any angle (see Fig. 4). Some menders dislike sand trays because in the event of a piece over-balancing, it can be quite maddening to have to remove every grain of sand from the adhesive before you can start again.

Larger pieces of china, such as platters and bowls, can be balanced in a cardboard carton in which newspaper has been crumpled up and stuffed, not only at the bottom but also on either side of the china as a support. This method has an added advantage in that if a piece overbalances, it should fall harmlessly on to the newspaper. Plasticine – the china mender's best friend – is another invaluable help in supporting china. Indeed, I often think that china mending could be summed up in three words, namely Plasticine, Patience and Practice. For instance, a knob of Plasticine on either side of a cup stops it rolling over while a broken handle is setting. Smaller objects can be stuck in Plasticine at any angle to achieve the correct balance (see Fig. 3), but if a broken edge is put in Plasticine, remember to degrease it before applying the epoxy adhesive.

As well as balancing the china one bit on the other, it is also necessary to keep the pieces in the correct position whilst they are setting. This is best done with gumstrip moistened in water. Cut sufficient pieces of suitable length and breadth. I use 1″ wide gumstrip and when applying the pieces over a curve I cut little nicks (about $\frac{1}{8}$″ is sufficient) to facilitate covering the bend – a dressmaker's trick. You also need to have a small bowl of water handy.

Sitting down comfortably at your bench or table, arrange yourself so that you have a lap on which to hold your china. I have a shelf under my bench on which I put my feet, but a footstool or bar would do as well. Your lap (clothed in an apron) is the best workbench available. It is a most sympathetic surface on which to handle china, as well as to catch any little pieces that may inadvertently drop off. This way the bench proper is left free for your tools and materials (see Fig. 2).

One last act is advisable before starting to stick – perhaps the most important. Fit the two pieces of china together *without* any

Figs. 3 and 4 Different ways of supporting china whilst adhesive is setting.

adhesive. Move them gently this way and that until the join is perfectly flush, *that is to say there is no ridge at any place along the length of the join on either* side and the piece, except for the line of the break, is as it was before it was broken. Doing this will tell you (1) If there are any old glue flakes left, and (2) what degree of invisibility of mend you can expect. Different kinds of pottery and china produce different kinds of joins. For instance, pottery, being soft, will probably crumble slightly at the edges when broken and the join will inevitably show, whereas a hard paste join (most continental and oriental china is hard paste) may well be nearly invisible.

Very occasionally the two parts of a broken piece of china appear to have 'warped' and no matter how hard you press you cannot achieve a ridge-free join. This is because some china is made under tension and when the tension is released it will spring apart and you are left to compromise as best you can – but it is far better to be aware of this situation before you apply the adhesive.

Your next step is to choose your adhesive. There are now several different synthetic resin adhesives from which to make your choice. For the last 18 years I have used Araldite and I can recommend it unreservedly for most repair jobs. Lately, however, other makes have made their appearance on the market and two of these I find useful for special occasions. The first is UHU Plus which at the time of writing is not on sale in this country, but if you can obtain some from Europe, it is worth including it in your equipment for the repair of multiple breaks. It is more 'runny' than Araldite and thus easier to spread and achieve a close join. It is also more expensive. The second is Super Epoxy, the adhesive and hardener of which are both clear. When mixed and applied to the broken parts which must be held together under pressure, it will set in only 10 minutes. This can be very useful for some jobs but it should not be used for multiple breaks. These three adhesives have slight technical differences which are stated in the instructions which accompany the packs and which the mender should note, but the method of use is basically the same.

Assuming that you have decided to use Araldite as being the best all-purpose cement, squeeze out equal quantities of each tube on to a clean and grease-free piece of glass, tile or saucer, remembering to replace the caps correctly. Mix them together with a clean penknife or similar tool. If the china you are sticking is white, add a little titanium dioxide powder to the mixture to offset the beige colour which is inherent in most epoxy adhesives. But do not add so much as to make it bulky and difficult to spread – practice will help you judge the right amount.

Simple Breaks

Now to carry out the most important part of china mending – that of obtaining a really good join. Let me say here and now that it is no good attempting any advanced work until you can achieve this, for not even the most skilful painting will disguise a bad join. On the contrary it will show up like a permanently sore thumb.

Small bowls and saucers are particularly good items on which to practise, as curved objects seem to lock together better and your hands fit round them easily. Cover one edge of the warm china with the adhesive, spreading it on as thinly as you dare. Beginners tend to apply far more than is necessary; experience again will tell you just how little you need. The only exceptions to this rule are (1) when the edges are damaged and then the adhesive helps to fill the gaps, and (2) when the edges are thick and craggy and application on one side only might not cover the surface sufficiently. Put the two pieces together as before, and adjust them, applying pressure evenly and as hard as you can until there are no ridges anywhere. You can use your thumb-nail, razor blade or penknife to test for this. They should be held together with just the thinnest possible film of adhesive. The pieces very often seem to slot in position almost like a jigsaw puzzle and sometimes a wriggle is all that is needed to get a completely flat mend.

When you think you have got the join as perfect as possible, apply the pieces of gumstrip, after you have dipped them briefly in water and shaken them out (not onto the adhesive). In the case of a plate, bowl or similar object, these gumstrips must be stuck on at right angles across the break, on both sides. Don't stint them but leave gaps so that you can test the join for adjustment if necessary. Cup handles and knobs should have the paper stretched across them and stuck down on either side – a criss-cross being made for extra strength if deemed necessary. Pat the gumstrip smooth with a rag – this also helps to dry off any excess moisture.

Sticking

When quite dry, the paper will shrink, thus exerting even more pressure, which is why it is important to get the 'pull' of the gumstrip in the right direction. Put the china in the prepared restbed and test the join for ridges in case it has moved (see Fig. 3). Sometimes it is useful to put a tricky mend in the restbed before perfecting the join, as this will allow you to use both hands and more pressure can be exerted. During these operations some excessive adhesive will have been squeezed out in between the gumstrips, and some will undoubtedly have been smeared on the surface of the china. Bearing in mind that the most important factor is not to disturb the accuracy of the join, you can deal with this as follows:

1 Remove it straightaway with razor blade, penknife or rag moistened in meths.
2 Leave it for 2 or 3 hours, when it will still be quite easy to remove, but the paper will have dried out and the adhesive will have started to set, so it will be easier to handle the china.
3 Leave it until the adhesive has set hard, when the china can be safely handled and it can be removed with glass paper and a razor blade. Full instructions on how to do this are given at the end of this chapter.

Whichever method you use, the following warnings should always be observed:

(*a*) Any gold decoration on the china must be cleaned with meths before the adhesive has set – gold is rather delicate and you could well remove it along with the adhesive if you leave it till later.
(*b*) Unglazed ware such as Wedgwood should also be cleaned up as soon as possible as set adhesive smears can be very tiresome to remove from this kind of china.
(*c*) Meths is a solvent of the adhesive before it is set, so avoid getting it into the joins as it could weaken them.

After 3 or 4 hours, look at your mends to see if they need adjusting. This can be done by heating the incorrect part by a radiator and pushing it into line – indeed you should have up to 12 hours in which to alter a bad join, but setting times can be accelerated by a warm room so it is safer not to leave it as long as this.

Details of these setting times are always included in the instructions with the two-tube packs. Full strength is usually reached in 3 days at room temperature and added strength of join is obtained by baking the china. One of the paints I recommend has to be baked at a low temperature and on those occasions the baking can be left until then. High oven temperatures could harm some china, particularly the more valuable pieces, so it is safer to stick to the lower temperatures. You should also check the accuracy of your domestic oven.

I consider that china that is going to be subjected to continual washing should always be baked.

A few additional aids to achieving a smooth join are:

1 Miniature bulldog clips or small carpenter's G-clamps for the edge of a plate or saucer (see Fig. 3).
2 Elastic bands to go round a bowl.
3 Small bags filled with sand or (if you can get it) lead shot – these can be put on tops of knobs or on fruit dishes that have come apart from their base.
4 Plasticine – very useful in supporting and wedging awkward pieces in place (see Fig. 4). But all of these must, of course, be applied correctly or they will do more harm than good.

Finally, finish the job by cleaning up your tools and mixing tile with meths before the adhesive has had a chance to set.

Multiple Breaks

When you are faced with a break of more than two pieces, you must first decide on the order of assembly. If practicable lay the china out on the table in front of you with the pieces in their correct places. You start the sticking process by choosing two pieces that fit easily and well with each other. Apply the adhesive and gumstrip and leave in a restbed as usual. Any adhesive that has spread on to a broken edge that is not being joined immediately must be cleaned off with a razor blade or meths before it hardens and hinders all subsequent joining. The remaining pieces are dealt with in a similar manner until the whole is assembled (see Figs. 5 and 6). If sufficient time is allowed for the gumstrip to dry slightly during the assembly, you should be able to handle the different pieces without overmuch disturbance of the joins. It

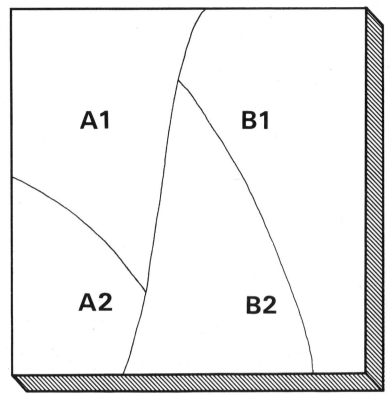

Fig. 5 Sequence of assembly for multiple breaks:
A1 to A2
B1 to B2
A1 and 2 to B1 and 2

is important that all pieces are fitted together before the adhesive has finally set because if you try to build them up in lengthy stages, however accurately you may think you have joined the pieces, you will surely find that one piece is slightly out of alignment and this can throw all the others out too. If you are pressed for time, you can compromise by fitting in the remaining pieces without adhesive but strapping them as usual with gumstrip. In this way you can ensure that the joins already completed are correct and the job can be finished later on. Another important point to remember when assembling a multiple break is to ensure that you are not left with a piece locked out, i.e. a piece that cannot be fitted in without disturbing the parts surrounding it (see Fig. 7).

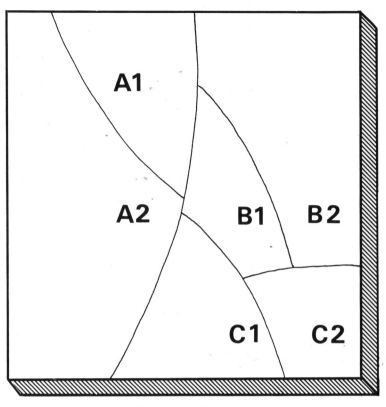

Fig. 6 Sequence of assembly for   Alternatively:
     multiple breaks: *A1 to A2*
    A1 to A2   *B1 to B2*
    B1 to B2   *C1 to C2*
    B1 and 2 to C2 and then to C1   *B1 and 2 to C1 and 2*
    B1 and 2, C1 and 2 to A1 and 2   *A1 and 2 to B1 and 2, C1 and 2*

If by chance you have let these parts set then you are in real trouble and your only solution is to apply a solvent, undo all your hard work and start again. Finally, do realize that the accurate joining of a badly broken piece of china is not easy and requires considerable practice, so don't be tempted to be too ambitious at first.

Sticking Cracked China

The repairing of cracked china crops up very frequently and so long as the crack has an open end, it is usually possible to make quite a good job. The same conditions of warmth and cleanliness

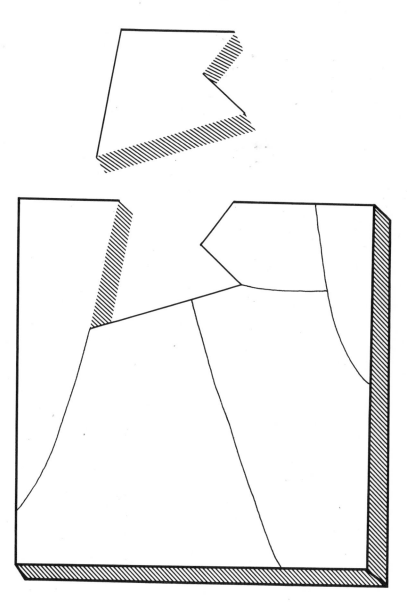

Fig. 7 Piece locked out during assembly.

are required, and adhesive, gumstrip, water and razor blade must be assembled. Taking the warm china from oven or radiator, gently insert the edge of the razor blade in the crack, just forcing it apart as recommended for cleaning (Chapter 1). This can be rather a nerve-racking operation, and rare indeed is the china mender who hasn't heard a fateful 'ping' which means that the crack has become a break.

Whilst the china is still warm, get as much adhesive as possible into the crack with a penknife or other suitable tool, covering it on both sides and working it against the slight ridge that will be caused by the enforced opening. When the crack is well filled, withdraw the razor blade and apply the moistened gumstrip on both sides – as for an ordinary join. When the adhesive has set, clean up, and, in the case of cups, bowls and vases, test for leaks.

Use of Powdered Pigments to Colour the Adhesive

When the edges of the break have become worn, it is sometimes helpful to tint the adhesive to match the china, in order to achieve a less noticeable join. White is obtained by the addition of titanium dioxide, while other colours can be achieved by the use of powdered pigments. Minute portions are added to the adhesive with titanium dioxide, if necessary. It is not easy to get an exact match, but even if it only tones in with the china, it is an improvement on the beige colour of the adhesive alone.

Cleaning up China when Set

When the setting time is completed, the china must be cleaned of excess adhesive from the joins as well as any general finger smears and the gumstrip.

First of all immerse the china in warm water and detergent and soak off the paper. This is especially important on any gold decoration – stripping off the dry paper would remove the gold with it. Take this opportunity to test the join. Ninety-nine times out of a hundred it will withstand firm pressure, but occasionally the mended piece comes away and must be re-stuck. If it is domestic china, such as a cup handle, I consider it should be tested in really hot water, and in my business, all domestic china is boiled for 5 minutes. This is not because I have no confidence in the adhesive, but because mistakes can be made and it is sometimes just not possible to get a dirty break completely clean and grease-free. Having dried the china, excess adhesive can be scraped off with a razor blade *after* you have rubbed it with a fine glass paper to break down the surface. Failure to do this could cause the glaze to come away with the adhesive – so tenacious is it. Smears are also rubbed away with fine glass paper until the whole surface of the china is clean and shining when scrutinized in a good light.

SUMMARY OF CHAPTER 2 ON STICKING

Requirements

Warm room, warm china.
Clean hands, clean china.
Dry china.

Method

1 Prepare gumstrips, water, suitable support (sand tray, plate rack, etc.).
2 Apply adhesive (mixed with titanium dioxide and/or pigments as necessary) to one side only, except on coarse pottery or damaged edges, when apply to both sides.
3 Press pieces together as hard and as accurately as possible.
4 Use meths to wipe adhesive off gold and unglazed ware before it sets.
5 When sticking multiple breaks, beware 'locking out' a piece and always join all pieces together (with or without adhesive) at one session.
6 Additional aids are: small bulldog clips, elastic bands, clamps, lead shot or sand bags, and Plasticine.

Cracks

Warm china, insert razor blade, fill with adhesive and apply gumstrip.

Cleaning up China after sticking

1 When set, soak in warm water to remove gumstrip. Rub excess adhesive with fine glass paper before scraping it with razor blade.
2 Test domestic china in hot water before use.

EQUIPMENT FOR STICKING

Item	*Stockists and/or Notes*
Glass, tile or saucer	On which to mix Araldite
Plate rack	
Sand tray	
Cardboard carton and newspaper	
Scissors	
Penknife with small blade	
Razor blade	
Cup of water	
Rag	
Elastic bands	
Lead shot or sand bag	
Plasticine	Should be of good quality such as Harbutt's
Epoxy adhesive	Ironmongers, stationers, D.I.Y. shop
Gumstrip	'Butterfly' brand is recommended
Methylated spirits	
Small carpenter's clamps	Tool shop
Miniature bulldog clips	Stationers
Titanium dioxide	Chemist – if possible buy a small quantity such as 100–200 grammes to start with
Kerocleanse	Alec Tiranti Ltd., 72 Charlotte Street, London W1P 2AJ
Pigments	See list of equipment for filling

Cleaning up when Adhesive has Set

Basin and warm water	
Towel	
Detergent	
Glass paper	Ironmongers – Oakeys Grade o or flour paper
Razor blade or craft knife	Craft knife need not be expensive

3 Filling Chips and Holes

In the course of my work, I find very few jobs that only require sticking. Almost every piece that I mend has a chip or hole that has to be filled.

Choice of Filler

A filler can be bought ready-made, such as Barbola, Sylmasta or Isopon, or you can make it up yourself. The one I recommend and which is hereafter referred to as epoxy 'putty', or 'putty', is made by mixing together an epoxy adhesive and titanium dioxide. This is similar to the procedure for sticking white china, but now much more of the powder is added. I prefer this to all others for the following reasons:

(*a*) It is dead white and the most china-like in appearance.
(*b*) It is very strong and waterproof.
(*c*) It sticks well to the china and to itself so that more can be added as necessary.
(*d*) It makes a good surface to which paint will adhere well.
(*e*) It can be coloured if necessary.

Unfortunately it is also very sticky, but the results are so good that it is worth while to persevere with its use.

Preparations

The rough surface of the chip or hole must first be cleaned and a grease remover applied if necessary. Next, you must examine the piece to be filled to see if a support is necessary – epoxy 'putty' tends to sag whilst setting, so it may be necessary to support it with a piece of Plasticine or gumstrip. If Plasticine is used it must be dusted with titanium dioxide to stop the 'putty' sticking to it.

Filling

Mix together equal quantities of adhesive and hardener and work in as much of the powder as you can with a penknife or palette knife. When you think you cannot work in any more and the result is still a sticky mess, cover it with the powder, then knead it with your fingers or rub it together in the warmth of the palms of your hands, from time to time dropping it into the powder so that more is absorbed and the putty gets stiffer and more manageable. Continue with this procedure until the result is quite stiff – only then is it ready to be applied to the china. Pat it into shape, not forgetting to copy any lines or mouldings on the china. Use a penknife that has been dipped in meths or titanium dioxide to do this. It is impossible for me to say when you should use one or the other – I find that I usually use the former method but if too much meths is applied, the putty will get too sticky – on these occasions use titanium dioxide instead.

When set, the putty has to be smoothed down to a perfect shape and surface with glass paper, so you must allow for this and apply a little in excess overall. But be careful not to overdo it or you will have a massive rubbing-down job on your hands. Examine the filling from all angles to make sure that you have followed the lines of the china. Even so there are few fillings that do not need to be 'patched' with a second or even third application of putty. A good test for a perfect filling is to close your eyes and move your fingers over the china and the filling – only when you cannot tell one from the other is your work ready for painting. A little titanium dioxide powder rubbed into the hands before handling the putty helps to reduce the stickiness whilst a rag dipped in meths is the best cleanser of the china, remembering particularly any gold decoration.

Pigments

Powdered pigments can be used to colour the putty as follows:

(*a*) On domestic china or earthenware that is subjected to frequent washing – such as tea or coffee cups, teapot spouts, lids, this takes the place of painting.

(*b*) To imitate unglazed china such as Jasper or Wedgwood.

(*c*) To act as a first coat of paint. Tinting the putty to tone with the china is very helpful in cases when too many layers of paint would stand out from the surrounding china – this is particularly so on Oriental ware with pale greeny, blue, or grey backgrounds.

It is not easy to get an exact match of colour with pigments, but even a toning-in is very often preferable to a coat of paint that may eventually discolour. Pigments can be mixed together and then mixed with the putty or they can be added separately as necessary. Only minute amounts are needed. Do remember to make a note of the colour(s) and shade(s) used for further patching if necessary. Oil paints can also be used to tint the putty, but the oil in the paint makes it more difficult to mix and the result will be less adhesive. A coat of adhesive under the putty will overcome this problem. Pigmented putty tends to set paler so allow for this.

Kaolin mixed with epoxy adhesive makes a beige-coloured filler which is not so adhesive but is far less sticky to use. It can be useful to imitate ivory.

French chalk and china clay can also be used as alternatives to titanium dioxide in a filler and are considerably cheaper, but this advantage is off-set by the colours of the resultant putties. French chalk is pale grey and china clay is a dark beige when mixed with an epoxy adhesive.

Rubbing Down

After 4 or 5 hours the putty will be half set and if desired, some of the excess can be removed now. Use a craft knife, razor blade or chisel for this. The latter can be made by grinding down part of an old hacksaw blade and giving the narrowed end a sharp bevelled cutting edge (see Fig. 8). When the filling is set quite hard, perfect it with glass paper, starting with a coarse one and finishing with the finest. A small round or half round rasp can be a useful tool too, but in the absence of a suitable file, a piece of glass paper wrapped round a pencil or similar object makes a useful substitute.

Always remember to rub excess putty off china with glass paper. Chipping it with a knife or razor blade could bring the glaze off with it, with a resultant pitted surface. Beware also of scratching the glaze with too coarse paper and remember that even the finest glass paper will scratch any gold decoration and also 'overglaze' enamels as found on Oriental china.

Shrinkage of Epoxy Putty

One slight disadvantage of epoxy putty is that it expands very slightly during heating and then contracts as it cools. Thus a filling stretching across a gap may sometimes show a tiny crack at the edges when it is baked after being painted with Chintex (see Chapter 6). This can be overcome either by using a cold setting varnish or by filling in the crack with a *very* thin mixture of epoxy putty and touching it up with a cold setting varnish. Be careful also to allow room for expansion if for any reason you need to fill a completely enclosed object such as the hollow branch of a candelabra. Failure to do so may cause the china to crack and even break.

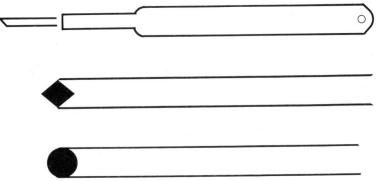

Fig. 8 Gravers and chisel.
Gravers *A wide range of shapes and sizes is available and they should be chosen or made to suit individual requirements. The following examples are considered to be the most useful and the dimensions are given as a guide. They can be made from old tools such as chisels and bradawls or masonry nails. These are cut as necessary with a hacksaw and ground to the shapes as shown in the diagram. A wooden handle – home-made or* bought *from an ironmonger – is fitted for ease of use.*
Lozenge or diamond
  Width 1.25, 1.50 or 1.75 mm
  Length 110 mm
Round
  Width 2–3.50 mm
  Length 80 mm
Chisel *Made from part of an old hacksaw blade. The narrowed end is ground down to a sharp bevelled cutting edge.*
  Length 127 mm
  Width 7.50 mm

SUMMARY OF CHAPTER 3 ON FILLING CHIPS AND HOLES

1 Clean chip or hole if dirty or greasy.
2 Mix Araldite and titanium dioxide to make stiff 'putty'. Add pigment if necessary.
3 If necessary apply Plasticine or gummed paper support.
4 Apply 'putty' to chip or hole and smooth down with knife dipped in meths or titanium dioxide.
5 On shallow chips, apply a layer of Araldite before the 'putty'.

Alternative fillers are Kaolin, French chalk or English china clay.

Rubbing Down Fillings when Set
When set, pare off any excess 'putty' with chisel or craft knife but only use glass paper to rub any 'putty' off glaze. Patch with more 'putty' as necessary.

EQUIPMENT FOR FILLING

Item	*Stockists and/or Notes*
Carbon tetrachloride	
Plasticine or gumstrip	
Meths	
Titanium dioxide	
Epoxy adhesive	
Penknife	
Mixing tile	
Rag	
Palette knife or penknife	Palette knife should be about 6″ (overall) and not too whippy
Kaolin French chalk	} Chemist
English china clay	The Fulham Pottery, 210 New Kings Road, London SW6 4NY

Powdered Pigments
Complete List to Cover Every Shade:

Titanium white	Raw sienna
Cobalt	Cadmium red
Cerulean	Light red
Burnt sienna	Alizarin crimson
Burnt umber	Viridian
Winsor lemon	Cobalt green deep
Aureolin	Ultramarine deep
Yellow ochre	Lamp black

Available from:
Winsor & Newton Ltd.,
51–52 Rathbone Place,
London W1P 1AB
The minimum quantity
on sale is 1 oz which is
far more than the
average mender needs.
Possible alternative
sources for the occasional
mender are:
(*a*) Paint merchants
(*b*) Fixed powder paints
from any art shop
(*c*) Chalk or pastels
ground fine

Equipment for Rubbing Down Fillings when Set

Craft knife
Home-made chisel
Razor blade
Glass paper

Needle files

Small rasp – round or half round

See Fig. 8

Oakeys Grade M2, F2,
No. o and flour paper
Ironmonger or tool
merchant. A round one
is the most useful, others
can be bought as
necessary
Tool merchant or iron-
monger

4 Moulds

When the missing piece needs to be shaped, either simply like the rim of a bowl or in a more complicated way such as an intricately carved handle, much time may be saved by taking a mould from an identical piece of china. This may be part of the original piece or it may be taken from a similar one, if you are fortunate enough to possess a twin. Moulds can either be pressed or cast. The former is achieved by pressing a moulding material on to a piece of china that is identical with the missing piece. A cast mould is made by enclosing the piece from which the mould is to be taken, in an open-topped 'box' made with Plasticine, which is then filled with a liquid material. These two kinds of mould can be filled either with a liquid material which eventually sets and makes a casting or with a plastic material which eventually sets and makes a pressing. I normally use the latter.

Pressed Moulds

In the case of the pressed mould, one of the best materials for the purpose is Plasticine, being inexpensive and easy to use. Let us imagine that you have to make a triangular piece of china, with sides approximately 2″ long, that is missing from a dish which has a fluted rim. First of all choose an identical part of the dish from which to take the mould. You must then decide whether it will be easier to take the mould from the inside or the outside, taking into account the necessity of filling it with epoxy putty later. In the case of the dish in question it is immaterial. You will need to count the number of flutings you have to reproduce and allow at least $\frac{1}{2}$″ on either side to fit it on to the dish in the correct position. Wet this piece of the dish to facilitate the removal of the Plasticine later. Knead a piece of Plasticine to remove lumps and lines and roll it out flat. It should be at least $\frac{1}{8}$″ thick and large enough to cover the area you have chosen. A jam-jar moistened with water makes a useful rolling pin in the absence of the real thing. Square off the uneven edges and place the Plasticine on the dish in the chosen position. Press carefully on to the china to reproduce the lines of the fluting and top edge of the rim – just overlap it here but not so far as to make it difficult to fill later. Remove Plasticine gently and place over the missing piece in correct position, i.e. matching flutings on either side. Keep it in position by pressing the outer edge of the Plasticine on to the china and hooking it over the rim on either side and pressing down (see Fig. 9). In order to prevent the epoxy putty from sticking, dust the Plasticine with a

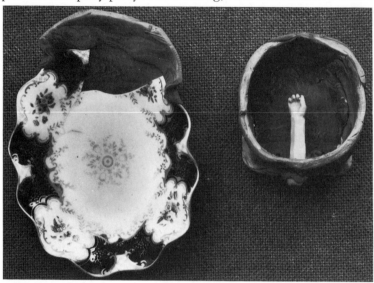

Fig. 9 Methods of making moulds: (Left) *Pressed Plasticine mould on fluted dish.* (Right) *Hand modelled in Plasticine supported in Plasticine box awaiting plaster of Paris mould.*

thin coating of titanium dioxide. An old paint brush is a help here. Now mix some epoxy putty and fill the mould, pressing it down gently into all the corners with a suitable tool dipped in meths or titanium dioxide. As in the case of a chip, you must allow for rubbing down with glass paper when set, so apply a little in excess on the inside. Leave to set. When the epoxy putty is hard, gently remove the Plasticine and perfect the shape with glass paper. It may be necessary to patch any imperfections with more putty.

Another useful material from which to make a pressed mould is Paribar. This is a dental wax which can be softened in very hot water. Beware of boiling it in a saucepan, however, as it will be extremely difficult to remove from the sides – instead pour near-boiling water over it and when softened, knead it with your fingers to remove lumps and creases. Apply to the china (which need not be wet in this case) in the same way as Plasticine and leave to harden, which it will do in a few minutes. During the setting time it remains sufficiently flexible long enough for you to remove it from the model, even if it has some undercuts.* It is much firmer than Plasticine and can be used over and over again and it is not necessary to dust it with titanium powder before applying the putty.

Cast Moulds

When it is desired to reproduce a more intricately shaped piece of china, be it a knob, handle or a new hand, you will need to take a moulding of the whole piece you are copying. In this case a pressed mould would be useless. It must therefore be cast in a liquid material which can either be rigid when set like plaster of Paris or flexible like Vinamold. If the piece being copied is very intricately designed with many undercuts, it would be impossible to remove a rigid mould from the model without risk of breaking it. In this case it is necessary to use a flexible material. If you are in doubt as to which to use, experiment with Plasticine. Press a size-able lump of it over the piece being reproduced. If you cannot withdraw it without distorting the Plasticine, you will have to use a flexible mould. Plaster of Paris is on the whole quicker to use than Vinamold, but the method of use is almost the same.

Rigid Moulds

Let us assume that you want to reproduce a handle on a bowl and you fortunately have another from which to take a mould. Although it is ornate, it has no undercuts and therefore plaster of Paris can be used. This will be a two-piece mould and you must first decide how it will be divided. Tip up the bowl on its side and prop it up. A sand tray, Plasticine and crushed paper may be needed here. Paint the piece to be moulded with a light oil to

* UNDERCUT = any hollow or cutaway in the modelling so shaped as to impede the lifting of the mould from it.

prevent the plaster from sticking to it. Now build up a container in Plasticine around the handle, into which the plaster of Paris can be poured. Roll out the Plasticine as you did for the pressed mould and construct the 'box', pinching the sides together to make it leak-proof. The walls of the box should be big enough and high enough to allow at least half an inch all round and above the handle. Plaster of Paris is always added to water so fill a small jug with sufficient to fill the mould and then add the plaster. Stir very gently to avoid forming air bubbles which would destroy the smooth surface needed for a perfect replica. Plaster must be kept dry, so use a different tool to ladle it out to that which you use for stirring it. The ultimate mixture should be as thick as whipped cream and the plaster starts 'working' as soon as water is added, so you should not be interrupted at this stage. Before actually pouring the plaster, jiggle and tap the jug on your bench to get rid of any air bubbles. Always pour the mixture in at one side of the container and not on to the model itself. This will push any trapped air ahead of it and explode it as it does so. Fill the container up to the halfway mark (or wherever it has been decided that the first part of the mould shall come to) and leave to set. This will take approximately 15 minutes. Before it has set completely hard, cut some 'keyways' into the sides of the mould. These are shallow scoops with sloping sides that get filled up during the pouring of the second half of the mould and will thus enable you to fit the two halves together quite accurately when set (see Fig. 10). Now you must paint the mould with the oil to avoid the second application of plaster from sticking to the first. Pour on enough to cover all the surface, not forgetting the keyways. Allow time for the oil to soak in – approximately 10 minutes. Now apply the top or second half of the mould, mixing and pouring on the plaster as you did for the first half. This must be allowed to dry out and harden thoroughly, which will take several hours – overnight if possible. When really hard, gently prise open the mould with a chisel or penknife at the joining of the two parts. In prising open the mould, care must be taken to avoid causing leverage on the china against which the mould abuts; thus the chisel should be inserted at a part of the join where the leverage on the opposite side is taken by the mould alone (see Figs. 11, 12, 13). The result should be a perfectly smooth and accurate two-piece mould.

Figs. 10–14 Different stages in making a plaster cast mould:
Fig. 10 The bottom part of the mould on the model, and the top part alongside. Note the keyways.

Filling the Mould

Before filling the mould it is necessary to gouge out a 'flash' groove, or escape channel all round the outer edge of the actual moulding (see Fig. 14). Any excess putty will ooze into this when the two filled halves are fitted together.

It is impossible to judge accurately the exact amount of putty required for each half of the mould, and rather than underfill them it is preferable to slightly overfill them. On fitting the two parts together, any surplus is squeezed into this channel where it forms a thin rim which can easily be cut off and filed flat.

Now cover both parts of the mould (not forgetting the 'flashes') with a thin coating of a parting or release agent to avoid the putty sticking to the plaster of Paris. This can be done more easily by gently heating the mould before applying the parting agent, which can then be smoothed on with a paint brush. Next fit the lower half of the mould on to the broken stubs of the bowl, propping it up on its side and holding it in place with the Plasticine container.

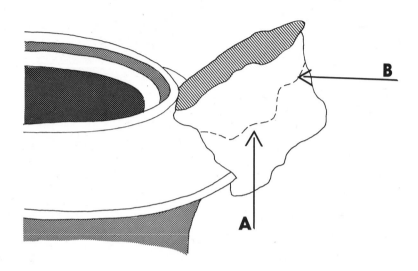

Fig. 11 Different places to open mould.
A *Correct.* **B** *Incorrect.*

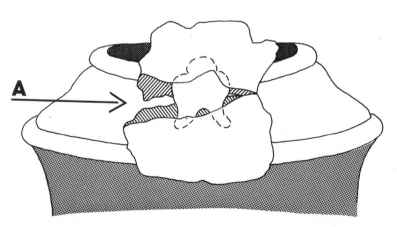

Fig. 12 **A** *shows the correct place to open a plaster mould; the leverage caused by the opening being taken by the mould alone, so that there is no danger of the handle being broken off. (See also Fig. 13, page 43.)*

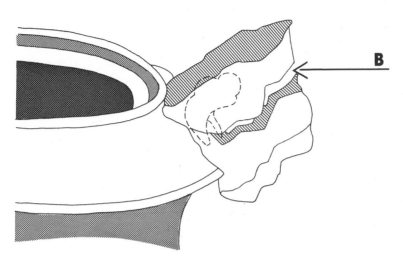

Fig. 13 **B** *shows the incorrect place to open the mould; the leverage caused by the opening being taken by the handle and that part of the bowl surrounding the handle. This could cause the handle to be broken off.*

Fig. 14 Bottom part of the mould in position on broken handle stubs with top part alongside. Both are filled with 'putty'. Note 'flashes'.

Fig. 15 New handle on bowl awaiting finishing touches.

Fill this part of the mould with putty, pushing it into all corners and crevices with a suitable tool dipped into meths. Now fill the top half in the same manner, remembering to leave room in the mould into which the broken stubs can fit (see Fig. 14). Finally place the top half on to the bottom half on the bowl and press hard on them. They can be kept thus with an elastic band or bound with string. Leave to harden, or if desired the setting time can be accelerated by baking in an oven. When ready, prise open the mould and perfect the pressing as necessary with glass paper (see Fig. 15). A rigid mould can be used for all Plasticine models – undercuts or no, as it is immaterial if the model is destroyed during removal from the plaster of Paris.

Plaster of Paris can also be invaluable when you wish to reproduce a delicately moulded leaf or flat rosette-type flower and you have a duplicate from which to take a mould. First paint the appropriate piece of china with oil, then make a stiff mixture of plaster of Paris and water and spoon it gently on to the leaf or flower. It should be about $\frac{1}{8}''$ thick to avoid breaking but it must not overlap the edges as this would make it difficult to remove. When set, remove the mould gently and fill with epoxy putty in the normal way. If it is desired to use the mould again, a release or parting agent must be applied to the plaster of Paris before filling with the putty.

Finally, beware of pouring plaster of Paris down the drain as it will set and cause a blockage.

Flexible Moulds

Should the piece of china from which you want to take a copy be so shaped that it would be impossible to remove a rigid mould from it without fear of breaking it, it is necessary to use a flexible moulding material (see Figs. 16 and 17). There are several of these on the market from which to choose. I prefer to use Vinamold 1028 made by Vinatex. Although the melting of this material is a rather lengthy process, this is offset by the fact that it can be used over and over again. The flexible moulds that are mixed in a matter of seconds, cost more initially and cannot be used again. Full instructions are given with Vinamold 1028 and the method of using it is the same as for a rigid mould except that (*a*) the model need not be oiled but should be warmed to avoid breaking when the hot liquid is poured on to it; (*b*) no parting agent is needed; and (*c*) flash grooves are cut in the form of narrow channels jutting out from the model (see Fig. 17). The moulding and shape of the bowl in the Figs. 17 and 18 allow the mould to be firmly fitted and held in the correct position on the broken handle stubs, thus obviating the need for keyways in this instance. When needed they can be cut with a razor blade. I melt Vinamold 1028 in a small saucepan with a lid, which I place on an asbestos mat over a gas ring.

Beware of making the walls of the mould too thin, as, being flexible, it could become distorted and mis-shape the epoxy putty. If a smaller quantity of titanium powder is used when mixing the putty, it will be less stiff and the above problem is not so likely to occur.

When you want to make a mould of a complete object on its

own – such as a hand modelled in Plasticine, it must be suspended in a Plasticine 'box'. You can do this either by (*a*) building in the handle by which you held it during modelling (see Chapter 5)

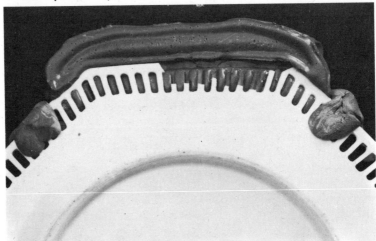

Fig. 16 Example of a flexible mould on an open work plate.

Fig. 17 Example of a flexible mould for the handle of a bowl.

Fig. 18 The new handle on the bowl. The original handle was not sym-metrical.

into one wall of the box, or (*b*) supporting it with two pins or matches according to size, piercing the opposite sides of the box and then the Plasticine model (see Fig. 9).

SUMMARY OF CHAPTER 4 ON MOULDS

Pressed Plasticine Mould

1 Wet part of china from which mould is to be taken.
2 Apply Plasticine (previously kneaded) and press well to obtain perfect impression.
3 Remove mould and fit gently over missing piece.
4 Dust Plasticine with titanium dioxide and fill mould with stiff 'putty', roll in hands if necessary.
5 Smooth down with knife dipped in meths or titanium dioxide.

Plaster of Paris Mould

1 Plan sections of mould.
2 Prop up china in correct position.
3 Paint china with a light oil.
4 Build up container.
5 Mix plaster to a rich cream consistency. Jiggle and tap container to explode bubbles.
6 Pour and ladle plaster in from one end so that trapped air will be driven out.
7 Allow to dry – about 10–15 minutes.
8 Cut 'keys'.
9 Oil plaster and allow to soak in.
10 Pour top half of mould.
11 Allow to dry.
12 Part mould into its two sections.
13 Cut 'flashes'.
14 Coat with release agent.
15 Fill with 'putty' and bind tightly.

Warning: Do not pour waste plaster down the sink or you will block the drain.

Flexible Mould

1 Plan sections of mould.
2 Build up container.
3 Melt pieces of Vinamold very slowly in saucepan with a lid.
4 Warm china model to avoid breaking it.

5 Pour on first half of mould.
6 Allow to set hard – preferably overnight.
7 Cut 'key ways' if needed.
8 Melt and pour on second half of mould.
9 When set, remove model, cut 'flashes' and fill with putty.

Warning: Do not make walls of mould too thin otherwise it will distort and alter shape of model.

EQUIPMENT FOR MOULDS

Item	*Stockists and/or Notes*
Water	
Mixing tile	
Plasticine	
Penknife or palette knife	
Epoxy adhesive	
Titanium dioxide	
Meths	
Dental plaster of Paris	Chemist
Chisel	
Any light oil or liquid detergent	
Old paint brush	
2 old spoons	
Sandtray	
Rolling pin	
Glass Paper	
Release or parting agent	I use Kiwi neutral shoe cream, but any furniture or shoe polish (preferably colourless) which does not contain silicones, is suitable.
Vinamold 1028	Order 1 lb from: Alec Tiranti Ltd., 72 Charlotte Street, London W1P 2AJ
Paribar dental impression wax	Claudius Ash & Sons Ltd., 26–40 Broadwick Street, London W1

49

5 Modelling

When it is necessary to make a missing piece and there is no duplicate from which to make a mould, the china mender has no option but to model it. This gives those with some artistic ability a chance to show their skill and it can be a most enjoyable process. It should be remembered that the artist on this occasion must not express his or her own style but that the style of the original modeller must be faithfully copied.

The china mender has the choice of two forms of modelling – direct and indirect.

Direct modelling is modelling in the composition of which the part is to be made such as Sylmasta or epoxy 'putty'.

Indirect modelling is making a model in a modelling material such as Plasticine and subsequently making a mould from it.

The china mender will normally use whichever method will achieve the best result in the shortest time.

Method and Equipment

It is impossible to give precise instructions on how to model. To my mind it is simply a matter of perseverance until the modelled part looks from all angles as if it was one with the whole piece. There are, however, a few tools and items of equipment which will greatly assist you in achieving a good result. First and foremost is a pair of dividers. With these you measure, measure and measure again, until the dimensions of the made-up piece are absolutely identical with the model. Calipers are another measuring aid. Boxwood and wire modelling tools are necessary for indirect modelling and a chisel and gravers for direct modelling. The latter can be home-made as was the chisel shown in Fig. 8, or can be ordered from a silversmith and jeweller's tool merchant.

China menders usually acquire their own favourite tools to fit a particular need. Amongst these might be discarded dentists' tools or a steel-ended leather work tool, as well as the ever useful chisel, small penknife or craft knife. Needle files and glass paper will be necessary too.

As regards the actual modelling materials, Plasticine or modelling wax is recommended for indirect modelling. In order to keep it clean and pliable, keep about $\frac{1}{4}$ lb of it in a plastic bag or other airtight container, especially for this purpose. Peach or white Plasticine is recommended for modelling limbs as this helps to simulate the real thing.

The items that require to be made up are usually those which stick out from the ornament, get broken off and are subsequently lost. The same ones tend to occur again and again and so after a time the china mender becomes quite expert at reproducing such things as cupid wings, hands and feet, ears of all kinds and parts of musical instruments. In the absence of another part of the ornament, take trouble in finding a picture or even a specimen of the real thing from which to copy. Apart from getting a true model, you will widen your interest in your work as a modeller. In my time I have visited a cowshed, gazed at a flock of sheep and even looked at 'Top of the Pops' to see how the musician's hand holds a guitar! Bird books and *The Observer's Book of Music* have been invaluable too.

Direct Modelling

Once again I prefer to use epoxy 'putty' as being the most durable of all compositions, although it is by no means the easiest to use. Make up a stiff mixture, allowing sufficient to make a handle by which to hold the model whilst you are working on it. This can be cut off later before fitting it to the piece of china. Now shape the 'putty', using a modelling tool or penknife, dipped into meths or titanium dioxide as necessary. It is difficult to achieve more than a very rough model at this stage, nevertheless it is important to get the right angle and size. Once the 'putty' has set or even whilst it is setting, continue to model, using chisel or craft knife and subsequently needle files, gravers and glass paper. It may be necessary to add more 'putty', not once but several times and it will certainly be necessary to use the dividers all the time. Only the mender can decide when to stick the new part on to the main piece and it may be easier to put the finishing touches when the modelled part is actually in position. The join must, of course, be made quite smooth so that, once it has been painted no hint of a made-up piece is visible.

I always keep any surplus pieces of epoxy 'putty', rolling them into small sausage lengths or shaping them in other ways. When set, these can serve as firm foundations on which to build up a hand or any other missing piece, thus saving both time and material.

Indirect Modelling

It is certainly far easier and more pleasant to model in Plasticine or modelling wax than to cut and file the hardened epoxy 'putty', but the necessity of making a mould and then filling it does entail a good deal of work. Proceed as you did for direct modelling, giving yourself a good handle by which to hold your work (see Fig. 9) and adding to or removing the modelling material until you are satisfied. It only remains for you to make a mould.

The following general remarks apply to both methods.

(*a*) Sometimes you will be in doubt as to the correct shape or even identity of the missing piece. Examine the china closely for any chips or unpainted patches as these will very often supply the answer. Bend a piece of roughly shaped Plasticine, this way and that until the best position is found, remembering always to examine the china from every angle. (*b*) Always remember that painting will blot out much of the detail and slightly increase the dimensions, so that if you model a hand a little on the large size, painting will make it more so, and if, for example, a hand is finely modelled, this must be over-emphasized in the built-up hand.

Hands

It is extraordinary how easy it is to give a hand six fingers, but if you shape the fingers all in one piece like a mitten, then make a cut down the middle and subsequently one on each side, you will avoid this mistake. Always put the thumb on as a separate piece afterwards, with the base of the thumb on the palm of the hand. This gives it a more natural appearance.

An alternative method is to shape the palm of the hand, and, from a long thin sausage of 'putty', to cut off short lengths for fingers. Then apply each one separately, merging them together later. Knuckles, finger nails and wristbone must be faithfully copied as necessary from the original.

Handles

All china menders will eventually be faced with the problem of making a new handle for a cup or jug. If the piece of china is for ornamental purposes only, a new handle can be made either by (*a*) making a mould from an identical cup or jug (this is by far the easiest and quickest method), or (*b*) modelling from an illustration or drawing by direct or indirect method.

Place a wedge of Plasticine shaped like the inside of the handle between the broken stubs and build up on to it with the modelling material. Whichever method is used, extra strength will be provided by applying some adhesive to the stubs *before* the handle is put on. Even so, when the job is completed the new part should be given a gentle testing in hot water.

If, however, the cup or jug is required for everyday use, I personally do not consider a made-up handle to be safe, unless it has the additional support of a wire core, the ends of which have been cemented into holes drilled into the china itself.

The mechanical side of china mending does not come into the scope of this book, but some menders may like to experiment by bending a piece of brass wire into the shape of a handle and sticking it on to the broken stubs. When set, a new handle can either be built up around it, or it can be set into a two-piece mould. The use of brass wire stuck on to the china with epoxy adhesive as a core around which to model may sometimes be of use on other occasions, when extra strength is needed to reinforce a particularly fragile piece such as the handle of a basket or the neck of a violin.

Teapot Spouts

Another common repair job is that of replacing missing and chipped ends of teapot spouts. These can be all shapes and sizes, ranging from sturdy family ones to the delicate piece that graces a china cabinet. The best method of building up a new one after cleaning off any stains, is to insert a sausage of Plasticine into the broken spout so that it protrudes well beyond the end. If both lips

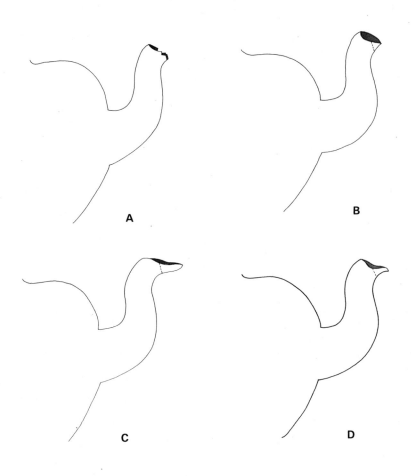

Fig. 19 Method of building up a teapot spout: (a) The broken spout. (b) Too short and wrong angle. (c) Too long and wrong angle. (d) Correct in length and angle.

are missing, you must use your judgement in guessing the correct length. In the case of antique teapots, it may be possible to find an illustration, for a reference. Bend the 'sausage' as necessary to continue the line of the spout. Dust the Plasticine with titanium dioxide before applying a stiff mixture of 'putty' and build up around the Plasticine. Model it into shape, your main concern at this stage being to continue the lines of the original spout when viewed from all angles. When set, remove the Plasticine and continue shaping with chisel, files and/or glass paper. Take care continually to study the outline of the spout as before, so that the made-up piece flows onwards from the china without interruption. The job may require several further applications of 'putty' and much gentle rubbing down before the new spout is the correct shape, size and thickness, but it is a satisfying job to have completed (see Fig. 19). If the piece is for everyday use, the inside of the pot should be left unpainted as the paint would not withstand the heat and staining of tea. Cabinet pieces or those for occasional use may be painted as usual.

Cupid Wings

The reproduction of cupid wings is one of the more lengthy jobs, often requiring much detailed modelling. Even if one wing still remains, it is of no use in the reproduction of the other by means of a mould. The following short cut does, however, slightly reduce the job time.

Moisten the existing wing with water to prevent sticking. Place a piece of Plasticine approx. $\frac{1}{4}''$ thick over one side of the wing. If the wing is curved, as is often the case, the concave side will be considerably smaller than the convex side and this should be taken into consideration and the dimensions checked with dividers. Carefully remove the Plasticine wing and gently bend it straight. Lay it on a piece of thin card and draw round it with a pencil. Cut it out and check for size and shape on the actual wing. Now mix some stiff epoxy 'putty' and dust the cardboard with titanium dioxide. Spread the 'putty' over the cardboard about $\frac{1}{8}''$ thick, bending it as necessary in the opposite direction of the existing wing. Fix it in this shape with Plasticine and leave to set. When hard, remove the cardboard, and, applying more 'putty', model the feathers on both sides, using the china wing as a model and checking all dimensions with dividers. Finally stick it on to the cupid and paint as usual.

Leaves

The easiest method of making leaves is by direct modelling. Start by making up some epoxy 'putty' and allowing it to harden for approximately 3 hours at room temperature or half an hour on a radiator. Roll it out to the required thickness by means of a small rolling pin or other round object, dusting it as necessary with titanium dioxide to prevent sticking. It should now be easy to handle. Using a sharp point, draw the leaf on the sheet of epoxy putty, then cut it out with a pair of small scissors. Leave to set and then stick it on as usual. Alternatively, place it in position on the ornament straight away, fixing it with a blob of adhesive and arranging it so that it lies in a natural position. Feminine ribbons that get broken off and lost can be made in the same way, and it is most encouraging to see how easily they can be made to fall naturally into place.

When it is desired to make a quantity of leaves, the mender may like to experiment, using a home-made tool that is similar to a pastry cutter and with which the leaves are stamped out. Much time can be saved by the use of this tool but the mender is warned that the initial making of the cutter can be both time-consuming and tedious.

First cut a strip of stiff aluminium foil from a pie case or cigarette pack. The strip should be approximately $\frac{1}{2}''$ wide and have perfectly straight sides. Start by measuring the distance from the base of the leaf where it joins the stem, to the tip of the first point. Allowing for a $\frac{1}{2}''$ handle with which to hold the cutter, mark this distance from one end of the strip and place it flat on the work table. Hold a chisel at right angles on the strip at the place marked and pull the remainder back over the end of the chisel. Turn the strip so that the formed part is nearest to you and measure the distance of the leaf from the first point to where it goes inwards. After marking this on the strip, repeat the pulling-back process against the end of the chisel. This is done more easily on the edge of a table or on a raised block of wood as it allows clearance for the formed part of the strip. Proceed in this way until the cutter is completed. When the leaf indentations are rounded, use a blunt-ended tool instead of a chisel to form the cutter.

Flowers

When a rigid or flexible mould is impracticable, whole flowers or just a missing petal can be made by cutting out the required shape in epoxy 'putty' in the same way as described for leaves, but the mender should be prepared for a very tedious and time-consuming job.

SUMMARY OF CHAPTER 5 ON MODELLING

Direct Modelling
Modelling in the composition of which the part is to be made, i.e. 'putty'.

Indirect Modelling
Modelling in Plasticine or modelling wax and then making a mould from that model.

Use dividers and calipers to measure.

When using Plasticine – model with boxwood and/or wire modelling tools.

When using 'putty' – make rough shape while 'putty' is soft – when hard, carve with craft knife, chisel, gravers, files and smooth with glass paper.

General Remarks

1 Make a good 'handle' by which to hold model.
2 Remember that painting will blot out detail and increase dimensions.
3 *Hands:* Don't make six fingers. Remember knuckles, finger nails and wrist bone. Put thumb on last.
4 *Teapot spouts:* Insert sausage of Plasticine in broken spout and build up round it, following lines of the spout.
5 *Cupid wings:* Copy shape of existing wing with Plasticine and cardboard. Dust cardboard with titanium powder and spread 'putty' over it. Bend to correct shape and leave to set. Remove cardboard and model the feathers as on existing wing, with more 'putty'.

EQUIPMENT FOR MODELLING

Item	*Stockists and/or Notes*
Epoxy putty	
Craft knife	
Glass paper	
Pair of small scissors	
Chisel	
Plasticine	White or peach, if possible
Dividers	
Callipers	
Boxwood modelling tools	
Wire modelling tools	
Needle files	
Gravers	H. S. Walsh & Sons Ltd., 243 Beckenham Road, Beckenham, Kent BR3 4TS Alternatively they can be home-made (see Fig. 8).

For Making a Leaf Cutter
Aluminium foil
Chisel

6 Painting

Let me start by saying that there is no point in your hoping that paint will cover up a mistake; rather will it help to reveal it. Most china menders find that painting is the most difficult part of their work at which to become really proficient.

Choice of Paints

First you must choose your paint, which ideally should have the following qualities:

(*a*) It should be absolutely clear and not discolour with age.
(*b*) It should be as hard as china.
(*c*) It should adhere well to the made-up surface.
(*d*) It should be resistant to hot water and liquid detergent.
(*e*) It should not be so quick setting as to disallow time for careful application and feathering at the edges.

These five conditions are a great deal to ask of any paint. It is possible to buy tins or tubes of paint of a wide range of colours and mix them as necessary. I consider it far better to invest in a selection of artists' oil colours (students' quality paints tend to be volatile) and mix them with a clear glaze or varnish to act as a medium.* A recommended list of colours will be found at the end of this chapter. These oil paints have been chosen not only for their ability to cover every combination of shade but also for their endurance and miscibility (i.e. ability to mix). Only in this way can you match the many different shades to be found on china. The medium that I prefer and which fulfils most of the requirements listed above is Chintex clear glaze. Its main drawback is that it is necessary to bake it, albeit at a low temperature, but even this is sufficient to darken the lines of epoxy adhesive of any existing joins. It also dries quickly, which necessitates working fast; however, practice should overcome this problem.

* *Chintex clear glaze:* a clear medium that requires baking. *Varnish:* a clear medium that is cold setting. *Enamel:* an opaque cold setting paint.

In view of this, I always suggest to beginners that they start painting with a cold setting medium. This is in any case a necessity in your equipment for use as follows:

(a) On pale coloured or white china when the darkening of previously mended joins would be undesirable.

(b) On china that has already been repaired by another mender and you cannot be sure that their methods and materials will withstand baking.

(c) On china that is too large to go into your oven.

(d) On stained and cracked china when even low heat might darken it or worsen the cracks.

(e) To reproduce fine lines or patterns, Chintex being too bulky for this.

(f) To avoid the tiny cracks which sometimes occur at the edges of a filling due to the contraction of the epoxy 'putty' after baking. (See Chapter 3, page 34.)

The small tins of clear Polyurethane such as Japlac or Humbrol fulfil most of the requirements and are inexpensive. Unfortunately they have a yellow tinge and tend to 'gel' unless all air is excluded from the container. Thus a certain amount of paint is always wasted unless it is decanted into progressively smaller containers.

A tin of white enamel of either of the same makes is also useful, not only as a basis for the imitation of white china but also, with the addition of the necessary tints, in matching other pale colours.

Before leaving the subject, I must mention three other cold setting varnishes that I am currently testing and which would appear to have great promise. The first is PU. II made by Furniglas Ltd. The makers state that it is water clear, has a glass-like hardness and exceptional resistance to solvents, heat and general wear. Its one disadvantage would seem to be that it is only sold in trade sizes of $\frac{1}{2}$ gallon and 1 gallon. The second is a clear Polyurethane finish made by Rustin's Ltd. They state that it is pale in colour and darkens very little on ageing. It is available from some paint shops or direct from the makers in $\frac{1}{4}$ pint and larger sizes. The third called Propol clear glaze is a two-part epoxy resin based coating. Equal parts by weight of the resin and hardener are mixed together and a diluent added as necessary. The makers state that it gives a clear, temperature-resistant waterproof finish to china and earthenware. Colour or pigments may also be added where these are required but a compatability test should be made prior to use. It is available in tins of 200 grams from Protective Polymers Ltd.

Choice of Brushes

The china mender will usually need three or four artist's sable hair (or a sable mixture) water colour brushes, but as these have now become rather expensive, the beginner should start with only one. As with tools, you will probably find your favourite, bearing in mind that the requirements of a brush are volume, strength and a fine point. Mine is a medium-sized one (Rowney's No. 3, series 34) and I find it ideal for a large proportion of my work. I also use a No. 1 and 2 and 4 of the same make and series for work not covered by No. 3. Your brushes must always be kept clean by immersing them in the appropriate solvent immediately after use, followed by washing them in soap and water.

Preparations

Before starting to paint, you must ensure that the surface is, and remains, free from all the little specks of dust and dirt that usually abound on most work tables. The area to be painted must first be brushed with a soft brush, and then, in the case of an initial surface or one that has been painted with Chintex, wiped over with a silk rag dipped into meths. In the case of an enamel-painted surface, cold water should be used instead of meths. Wipe your paint saucer with meths and examine your paint brush for flecks of dust and old paint. It is a good idea to have different brushes for different mediums and yet another old (but not cheap and hair shedding) brush with which to mix the paint.

Now decide which colours you are likely to need and squeeze sufficient (a dab is usually enough) on to a piece of paper. This paper should be fairly absorbent but not hairy. The paper will absorb some of the oil in the paint, which is helpful when you are using Chintex which has a synthetic resin base; also it is often possible to use the same dab of paint for two or three days, which is a useful economy.

Sufficient practice will enable you to match colours quite quickly, so that in time you will be able to look at the china and decide at once which colours you will need. But beginners will have to experiment at length to achieve the right shade. If you have difficulty in matching a colour, a good tip is to try changing the combination of paints and use different ones to achieve a similar but more exact result.

Painting with Cold Setting Medium

Now you are ready to start painting. Assuming that you are using Humbrol as a medium, start by ladling sufficient of it into a paint saucer with a palette knife. If you consider it is too thick, thin it with a few drops of turps. Now add your colours, mixing them as necessary with your old brush. A dab of the resulting colour alongside the colour to be copied is a useful test for accuracy of match. As with modelling, it is difficult to give detailed instructions on how to paint, but I find that, as a general rule, beginners tend to be too finicky and to stint the paint. Be quite bold and apply it with even strokes to cover the surface. It is on reaching the edges that the really tricky part occurs. Here the artist must 'feather' or graduate it so that the joining of the made-up part with the china itself is rendered as invisible as possible. This is one of the most difficult things to achieve, but do persevere with it because failure to do so will nullify all your hours of careful sticking and building up.

When the whole surface is evenly covered, clean your brush of excess paint by wiping it on a rag or on the rim of the paint saucer. Now apply it to the edges of the painted area to absorb and attenuate the ridge that will have formed. Continue feathering by mixing a little of the paint with a few drops of turps or white spirit and applying it also to the edges, followed by some more strokes with a brush cleaned of surplus paint as before. Thus the painted area gradually fades away altogether. But in doing so you must not encroach on the china beyond the absolute minimum. The overpainting should always be confined as far as possible to the made-up surface and not spread far beyond it as is so often done. For instance, the overpainting of a new hand should stop at the break and not extend all the way up the arm to the sleeve.

Finally thoroughly clean your brushes and paint saucer with the appropriate solvent.

Painting with Chintex

The preparations for painting with Chintex are similar to those for painting with a cold setting medium. Although it is possible to obtain a jar of special thinners from the same firm this should not be necessary unless it is desired to reproduce a thin, washy finish or to use up some of the last drops in the jar which have become thick and tacky. On receipt of the glaze you should make sure that it is quite thin and runny. Acetone or amylacetate is the solvent for this paint, so have some handy for cleaning your paint brushes and paint saucer on completion of the job.

Apply the paint as before but now you will find that you must work more quickly to complete the job before the paint gets too tacky to use. The addition of a little extra Chintex either in the paint saucer or on the china can defer this moment, but an over-generous amount on the china will cause it to run in droplets.

An overwarm room will hasten the setting time as will working by an open window on a breezy day.

Owing to its bulky nature, feathering with this glaze is an even more difficult process than with an enamel, and beginners should not be discouraged by initially poor results. This is especially so on china with a pale background and high glaze, when the ridge of the join between the paint and the china causes a reflection through the glaze that is very hard to disguise. Your only way of doing so is to apply a little *clear glaze* medium at the edges and merge it with the paint with short feathering strokes. The application of thinned Chintex is not advised in the same way as was done when feathering with an enamel.

Each coat of Chintex must be baked at 220°F for at least 20 minutes, allowing extra time for the china to heat up.

Finally, thoroughly clean your brushes and paint saucer.

The following general instructions apply to both mediums.

Number of Coats to Apply

It is impossible to lay down any hard and fast rules regarding the number and colour of coats of paint to apply, but except for the very small touching-up jobs that extend only for a centimetre or two, it is seldom that a single coat will suffice to disguise a made-up piece. The following rules are offered as a rough guide:

(*a*) If the china is coloured, the first coat will be a rich mixture and be white or have a great deal of white in it. This is to give body to the paint which would otherwise be transparent, the colour showing darkest where the paint lies thickest. Owing to the high proportion of paint to medium, this coat may have a matt finish when it dries. The second coat will match the ultimate colour and be less rich, with less or no white in it. The third coat will have no white in it and will match the ultimate colour.

(*b*) If the colour of the china is translucent and has a luminous quality shining through the paint, the first coat will be white followed by two coats of matching colour.

(*c*) If the china is a dark, dense impenetrable colour, all coats will be mixed to match this colour.

Finally, apply a protecting coat of clear glaze or varnish. This is particularly necessary in the case of domestic china. Each undercoat must be allowed to dry thoroughly, or, in the case of Chintex, baked for the necessary period. It must then be rubbed down gently with flour paper to remove any imperfections and wiped over with meths or cold water as appropriate, in preparation for the next coat.

Matching Colours

The dark blue colour as found on Worcester china can be matched with a coat of white followed by one or two coats of ultramarine to which a little crimson lake has been added.

A flesh tint is best matched with a first coat of white to which a little Payne's grey and Naples yellow has been added, followed by a coat of light red or burnt sienna.

White china is one of the most difficult to copy. White paint alone is never sufficient to achieve a good match as will be evident if a dab of white is put alongside some white china. It is usually necessary to add a little of either Payne's grey, cerulean or cobalt blue or chrome green. Apply two or three coats as necessary. The final coat will probably only need very little or no white in it and will act more as a translucent overglaze, through which the undercoat shines.

Crackle or Crazing

When the glaze on a piece of china is criss-crossed with a network of fine lines, it is called 'crackle' or 'crazing' and the china mender will occasionally be called upon to copy it. This is best done by drawing the lines with a sharp-pointed medium hard pencil and then lightly applying an overglaze. It is advisable to practise this before trying it on the china itself.

Matt Finish

When the china is unglazed or has a matt finish and pigments have not been used to produce this effect (see Chapter 3, page 32), it will be necessary to paint it on. This can be done either by using a matt varnish or by mixing the oil paints and clear medium as usual and then adding a little talcum powder and mixing it well before applying it to the china.

Fine Lines and Patterns

If the use of an enamel and a fine brush is still too clumsy to produce lines of the requisite delicacy, the mender should resort to the use of waterproof ink and draw the lines in with a medium fine nib (not a mapping pen). Allow to dry thoroughly and then apply a coat of clear glaze or varnish.

Electric Light

This causes certain colours, notably green and blue, to change quite considerably, for which reason menders should only paint in daylight, unless the china is to reside permanently in a lighted cabinet.

Finally, it must be remembered that the durability of a painted surface depends a great deal on the atmospheric conditions in which it is kept. Thus a pale-coloured repair job will last very much longer in a china cabinet than on a mantelpiece above a fire. Made-up pieces on domestic china that is subjected to constant washing must also be expected to lose their gloss and discolour to a certain extent.

Using an Airbrush (fine paint spray)

The disguising of cracks and of the join between the made-up piece and the china, can be very satisfactorily achieved by use of an airbrush.

These are expensive to buy and require considerable practice to use efficiently.

SUMMARY OF CHAPTER 6 ON PAINTING

Paints

For preference use artists' oil paints mixed with Chintex (which needs baking at 220°F) or a cold setting clear varnish.

Brushes

Artists' sable water colour brushes.
Requirements are: volume, strength and a fine point.

Method

1 Dust china with a soft brush.
2 Wipe with a silk rag dipped in meths (or water when painting with enamel).
3 Have clean saucer and clean brushes.
4 Squeeze colours on to pad of paper or on to side of saucer.
5 Apply as many coats as necessary, rubbing down in between each coat with flour paper.

General Instructions
If China is a Pale Colour

First coat will be rich and be all white or have a great deal of white mixed in it.

Second coat matches ultimate colour and will be less rich with less or no white in it.

Third coat will have no white in it and will match the ultimate colour.

If China is a Dark Colour but Translucent

First coat will be white followed by two coats of matching colour.

If China is a Dark, Dense Impenetrable Colour

All coats will be mixed to match this colour.
Final coat for all will be a clear varnish or glaze medium.

Warning: There is no hope of the paint covering up a mistake, rather will it help reveal it.

EQUIPMENT FOR PAINTING

Item	*Stockists and/or Notes*
Turpentine	
Pad of paper	
Silk rag	
Meths	
Soft brush	
Glass paper	
Paint saucers	Plastic ones with three divisions are very useful
Paint brushes	Rowney's No. 1, 2, 3, 4 in series 34
Chintex clear glaze	1 oz or 4 oz pot from Chintex, Wraxall, Bristol BS19 1JZ
Acetone	
Cold setting varnish:	
Humbrol, Japlac	Paint or craft shops
PU II	Furniglas Ltd., 136–138 Great North Road, Hatfield, Herts
Rustin's clear polyurethane finish	Rustin's Ltd., Waterloo Road, Cricklewood, London NW2 or paint shops
Propol clear glaze	Protective Polymers Ltd., Rhee Valley Works, Shepreth, Royston, Herts SG8 6QB
Paints	Small tubes of artists' oil colours. Available from: Winsor & Newton Ltd., 51–52 Rathbone Place, London W1P 1AB (or artists' supply shops)

Recommended List

Titanium white	Burnt umber	Crimson lake
Payne's grey	Raw umber	Rose madder
Ivory black	Naples yellow	Cadmium red
French ultramarine	Winsor lemon	Indian red
Cobalt	Aurora yellow	Viridian
Cerulean	Yellow ochre	Cobalt green (deep)
Burnt sienna	Raw sienna	Permanent green light

7 *Applying Gold Decoration*

The china mender is very often required to reproduce some gold decoration, and there are four different ways in which he or she can do this, the choice being dictated by the type of china and the use to which it will be put:

1 *Treasure Gold liquid leaf.* This is an excellent general-purpose gold paint. Although I have not been using it for long, I find it stands up very well to general wear and tear. It is extremely easy to apply, the user only having to give the bottle a good shake before he or she proceeds with the painting. There are several shades of gold as well as silver and copper. I find Classic is a good match for most jobs. It is rather expensive but will last a long time. A protective sealer is available which can also be used if an over-glaze finish is required.

2 A *bronze powder* of superfine grain used with Chintex clear glaze as a medium. This is recommended when the requirement is for a paint that will stand up to a good deal of washing. The most important factor in applying bronze paint is to seal it with a final coat of clear glaze which is baked on. Failure to do this will cause it to discolour and turn green in time.

3 *Raw umber* mixed with a medium is also surprisingly like gold paint and can be very useful in reproducing a pattern, although it is not suitable for covering large areas.

All these are applied in the same way as other paints, any pattern being drawn on beforehand with a Chinagraph pencil.

Very fine lines are best painted with a cold setting medium, Chintex being too bulky for this type of work.

4 The application of *gold leaf* is another way in which gold can be copied but as it is a more lengthy and expensive method, the china mender will probably reserve it for the more valuable pieces he or she is called upon to repair. The gold leaf I recommend is applied by means of a transfer which is pressed on and adheres to the china in those places on which a size has been painted. Gilding is always the last process before a final coating of clear glaze.

The method of use is as follows: First ensure that the background paint is completely dry, then wash the china in cold water and dry it with a rag (preferably silk) in order to remove any dust. Now choose your size. Once again you have the choice of Chintex clear glaze or a cold setting varnish, the first being preferred as usual when wear and tear is a consideration. It is also quicker to use. Proceed by cutting the transfer leaf into narrow strips as necessary – $\frac{3}{4}''$ is a useful width. Ladle the size on to a clean saucer with a clean palette knife and mix in a little ivory black oil paint. This will enable you to see where you have applied the size. Draw the lines or pattern with a pencil as necessary and paint on a thin application of size, overlapping the pattern for a short distance before easing off. Put a small dab of size somewhere on the china to act as a test strip. Defer applying the transfer until the size is *just* tacky – this is a matter of 10–15 minutes (depending on the room temperature) in the case of Chintex and several hours in the case of a varnish. Use the test strip to decide the right moment, then press the transfer, gold side down, on to the size and rub with the fingers. After a few moments, remove the paper and the gold pattern should remain, albeit very blurred. This can be cleaned up by dusting it with a soft brush, when all the loose particles should come away. Painting mistakes are best corrected by the gentle use of a sharpened piece of wood, such as an orange stick, that has been dipped in water. Another application of gold leaf may be necessary, and this is applied in the same way as was the first. If Chintex is used as a size, it is baked as usual. Before applying the final protective coat of clear glaze or varnish, gold leaf should be burnished. This can be done in two ways, first by placing a small piece of celluloid on the gold and rubbing it with the back of a spoon-shaped tool – I use a leather work tool; or alternatively, if it is a rounded surface, by polishing it with a strip of transfer paper, which you hold at both ends and see-saw up and down.

Finally, the artist should be warned that it is well-nigh impossible to copy satisfactorily the brassy gold decoration that is found on much china.

SUMMARY OF CHAPTER 7 ON APPLYING GOLD DECORATION

Treasure liquid leaf, bronze powders and clear glaze medium and raw umber are all painted on in the normal manner.

Gold Leaf

1 Wash china in cold water and dry with a silk cloth.
2 Cut transfer leaf into strips.
3 Mix a little black paint into size.
4 Paint lines or pattern also test strip.
5 When *just* tacky, apply transfer.
6 Clean up with a soft brush and correct mistakes with peg wood.
7 Burnish.
8 When completely dry or baked (in the case of Chintex) apply a second coat if necessary.
9 Apply a final protective coat of clear glaze or varnish.

EQUIPMENT FOR APPLYING GOLD DECORATION

Item	*Stockists and/or Notes*
Treasure gold liquid leaf	Art shop
Bronze powders	Alec Tiranti Ltd. or Winsor & Newton Ltd.
Raw umber	
Gold leaf	I prefer single fine transfer gold leaf. Available from: George M. Whiley Ltd., Victoria Road, Ruislip, Middlesex HA4 0LG
Chintex or clear varnish	
Black paint	
Soft brush	
Orange stick or peg wood	

Item	
Burnishing tool and piece of celluloid	Paint saucer
	Meths
Silk rag	Turps
Palette knife	Acetone

8 Glass

The repair of glass is often considered to be more difficult than mending china. I personally do not find this to be so, although it is not possible to effect such a wide range of repairs. This is mainly due to the delicate nature of glass and the fact that small cracks caused at the time of the original break tend to flake off as chips, with the result that the glass breaks in a new place. This occurs very often with wine-glass stems and for that reason it is usually a waste of time to try to mend them unless they happen to be thick and the bowl will balance on the stem. Even then the owner should be warned of the possibility of a re-break with dire consequences. Fortunately, such objects as bowls, vases, decanters and the circular base of wine glasses can often be put back into service for many years, and if they are of cut glass, the join should not show overmuch.

Cleaning

The glass should be cleaned up as usual, but when washing it take care to ensure that it is first put into warm water before you add any hot. Do not clean it with anything abrasive, but if you add a little meths to the rinsing water, a nice sparkle will result. Distilled water is another excellent cleanser.

Sticking

Glass is stuck with the same adhesives, used in much the same way, as china, the main difference being that unless the adhesive and hardener are both clear, like Super Epoxy, a little silver bronze powder, and possibly a little titanium dioxide, should be added at the time of mixing. This is to offset the beige colour of the adhesive. It is not necessary to warm the glass beforehand, and it is advisable not to bake it afterwards – coloured glass must *never* be baked. The beginner may find it more difficult to achieve a perfectly flush join, as glass has no grain in which to 'slot' it, but as before, 'practice makes perfect'. Apply gumstrips and balance it on a restbed as usual. When the adhesive has set, wash off the gum-strip and clean smears off the glass with fine-grade wire wool which has been dipped into soapy water. Incidentally, it is worth noting that Brillo soap pads are made from standard (or medium) grade steel wool: I have used them successfully on occasions when I have run out of the finer grade, but it is advisable to experiment with a test patch on the underneath of the glass, scrutinizing it for scratches with a magnifying glass before proceeding further.

Cracks

Owing to its intractable nature, it is not possible to repair cracked glass with an adhesive, but I have mended a leaking vase success-fully by sealing the crack with a thin 'sausage' of epoxy 'putty' rolled out and pressed firmly on to the glass with a tool dipped into meths.

Fillers

At the time of writing I know of no filler both practical to use and water clear, that can be used to replace large pieces of missing glass. But the advantages and disadvantages of the different compositions available are listed below for experimentally-minded menders.

Acrylic resins. Acrulite has a yellowish tinge which tends to increase with age. It can be tinted with the addition of a little oil paint to match coloured glass and is easy to mix. It can be used with a Plasticine mould, but it sticks to plaster of Paris. In view of its comparatively limited use by the average craftsman, it is rather expensive. Instructions for mixing come with the pack.

Technovit 4004a. This consists of a powder which is mixed with a liquid. The makers think that it will set water clear if the utensils are kept scrupulously clean, but it is much more expensive than Acrulite.

Polyester casting resins. These set absolutely clear, but the minimum retail quantity is 1 lb and they have a shelf life of only approximately six months. They are quite expensive and rather complicated to use. They can be coloured with the addition of oil paints.

Super Epoxy adhesive. This can be used to fill small holes and is absolutely clear initially, although it may yellow in time, depending on the exposure to heat and sun. It sets hard in 10 minutes. When mixing, stir slowly and gently to avoid air bubbles. Colours can be introduced by the addition of a small quantity of oil paint. Sellotape or gumstrip can be used as a backing or support whilst setting. It must be shaped as far as possible before it sets, as rubbing down with sandpaper will scratch it.

Epoxy 'putty'. The only other substitute for glass, albeit a very poor one, is epoxy 'putty' applied in the same manner as for china and subsequently painted silver. Care must be taken not to scratch the glass when rubbing down the filling.

Rubbing Down Sharp Edges

The mender is sometimes asked to rub down a sharp or chipped glass edge. This can be done with a fine India or carborundum stone. It should be dipped in water and the glass rubbed gently with it. This rubbing will produce a matt or finely scratched finish, but this is unavoidable and at least it will prevent a cut hand or mouth. The stone can also be used to rub down china for such reasons as to remove the stubs off a handleless mug to convert it into a vase, but this can be a very lengthy process.

SUMMARY OF CHAPTER 8 ON STICKING GLASS

1 Wash in warm water and detergent.
2 Mix epoxy adhesive as usual and, unless using Super Epoxy, mix in a little titanium dioxide and silver powder.
3 Spread thinly on to one of the broken edges of glass.
4 Apply gumstrips and balance in restbed whilst setting as for china.
5 It is not necessary to bake glass, and coloured glass must never be baked.
6 Clean up with fine-grade wire wool, NOT glass paper.
7 Add meths to the final rinsing water to give a sparkling finish.

EQUIPMENT FOR GLASS MENDING

Item	*Stockists and/or Notes*
Warm water and detergent	
Meths or distilled water	
Epoxy adhesive	
Silver bronze powder	Alec Tiranti Ltd.
Florescan Silver Bronze colours	Winsor & Newton Ltd.
Titanium dioxide	
Mixing tile and tool	
Gumstrip	
Bowl of water	
Suitable restbed	
Fine grade wire wool	
India or carborundum stone	Tool shop

Fillers

Transparent Acrulite No. 154	Rubert & Co. Ltd., Acru Works, Demmings Road, Cheadle, Cheshire SK8 2PG
Technovit 4004a	
Polyester casting resin	Alec Tiranti Ltd.
Super Epoxy adhesive	Ironmonger, or D.I.Y. shop

9 Professional China Mending

By the time you have mended all your own broken china, you may have become so interested, practised and skilled in the work that you will want to start a small business. If you do, I hope that the following notes will be helpful.*

Records of China Under Repair

Experience has taught me that the following records are essential for the smooth running of a business. Each item of china should be entered in a book with:

1 A serial number. I start with number 1 on the first of January each year. This number is for identification purposes and should be written with a Chinagraph pencil on the main piece of the china.
2 The name and address of the owner.
3 The date it was brought in.
4 A description of the piece in sufficient detail to be able to distinguish it from any other.
5 A record of the number of broken and missing pieces.
6 Any special remarks.

SAMPLE ENTRY IN CHINA RECORD BOOK

Mrs S. Masher,   *Nos. 192–194*
Broken Hill,   *16 June 1974*
Stikney

192   Blue and white breakfast cup, willow pattern. Replace handle.
193   1 teaplate, green with white spots, in 3 pieces.
194   1 Chelsea Derby Cupid. Make new wing.
  Customer cannot collect until September.
  Cost. . . . .

* I recommend advanced china menders, and especially those who wish to take it up professionally, to read *China Mending and Restoration* by C. S. M. Parsons and F. H. Curl, published by Faber.

It is best to seek the advice of a professional as regards the accounting side of the business and he will tell you what account books he would like you to keep.

You can either charge your customers on a time basis or work out a set price for the different types of mends. In my business I use a combination of both. I have set prices for the domestic china with their usually standard types of breaks, and I keep special time sheets for the more valuable ornaments and decorative china.

Do remember that you can always increase your charges more easily than you can decrease them.

Do examine and discuss the job with the owner whenever you can. I have so often been assured that all the pieces were present, only to find that some were missing when I came to fit them all together. Until I learnt better, I would spend hours groping on the floor and searching the wrapping paper, thinking that the fault was mine.

Do keep the broken pieces in a container of some kind.

Do consult an insurance expert regarding your position in the case of loss of, or damage to, the china through fire, burglary or further breakage. You must make it clear to your clients that although every care will be taken of their possessions, all repairs are at owners' risk.

If you consider that the job is going to be very expensive, inform the owner and give an estimate if required. As it is difficult to assess accurately the completion time of a job, and in order to allow for unforeseen difficulties, it is advisable to give a minimum and maximum price. It is no exaggeration to say that realistic costing is usually achieved by doubling the expected job time. The owner will appreciate the warning and I find that it is very seldom that a job is withdrawn as a result. Give warning also of any special aspect of the job, such as difficulty in completely disguising a join.

Finally, if you want to avoid the sordid question of money altogether and yet receive a reward for your labours, ask for a bottle of some kind in payment. This can vary with the job, such as some bottles of beer for a cup handle and half a dozen bottles of champagne for a new hand on a Meissen figure!

Index